Sin is Serious!

Jesus says, "For I did not come to call the
righteous but sinners to repentance".
Ben Thomas (Fisher of men)
Telephone: 01633 894447
Email: benjam.halleluja@virgin.net

Sin is Serious!

**A simplified version of
The Plague of Plagues   a Treatise on Sin
by Ralph Venning, first published in 1669**

The full version, under the revised title of
The Sinfulness of Sin is available from the Banner of
Truth Trust, 3 Murrayfield Road, Edinburgh EH12 6EL

Prepared by

John Appleby and Peter King

GRACE PUBLICATIONS TRUST
175 Tower Bridge Road
London SE1 2AH
England
e-mail: AGBCSE@AOL.com

Joint Managing Editors:
T.I. Curnow
D.P. Kingdon M.A., B.D.

Consulting Editor:
J. Philip Arthur M.A.

ISBN 0 946462 690

© Grace Publications Trust 2004

Distributed by:

Evangelical Press
Faverdale North Industrial Estate
Darlington
DL3 0PH

Bible quotations, unless otherwise indicated, are taken from the HOLY BIBLE, NEW INTERNATIONAL VERSION. Copyright c 1973, 1978, 1984 by International Bible Society. Used by permission of Hodder & Stoughton, a member of the Hodder Headline Group. All rights reserved.

Cover design and artwork by Lawrence Littleton Evans
Printed in Great Britain by Creative Print and Design (Wales), Ebbw Vale

Contents

Page

Preface	7
Introduction	11
1. What is sin?	15
2. The sinfulness of sin	17
3. Witnesses to the harmfulness of sin	43
4. The usefulness of understanding the nature of sin	71
5. Things we can learn from the fact that sin is our enemy	83
Advice to those who are not yet Christians	89

Preface
(to be read first)

THE LAST CENTURY has seen two terrible World Wars take place, lesser regional and tribal conflicts all over the world, a genocidal holocaust, brutal dictatorships rise and fall, ethnic cleansings, huge famines, horrendous floods, and world wide diseases like AIDS sweeping the nations with devastating effect. We are waking up to the fact that *there is such a thing as evil in our world.*

CURIOUSLY, throughout this same period, there has been a growing refusal to believe in the reality of what the Bible calls sin. The old Ten Commandments of the Bible are regarded more as Ten Suggestions which you can now a days safely ignore. Can it be that as general belief in what the Bible says has diminished or even been rubbished by some the evidence that there is evil in the world begins *to stare us in the face?*

BUT *WHY* is our world not perfect? Come to that, why are we not better than we are? There s only one reasonable answer to this, and it is the Bible that brings it to us. Evolution doesn t give us the answer things *aren t* slowly changing for the better; there s more wickedness in the world now than ever there was. Other religions don t provide answers. Some suggest there is no such a thing as sin anyway, so why bother? Others suggest that if there is such a thing as wickedness in the world, we can cure ourselves of it   despite the fact that our news media bring us evidence that *we are not making ourselves better*. So we face a human dilemma.

THE BIBLE EXPLAINS that evil came into the world because the first people God created to live in his perfect world and care for it, decided they didn t want to live the way he advised and they rebelled against him. Ever since then that attitude of not wanting to do what God says has become everyone s *natural* attitude. We are all born with it. *And it gives rise to every wrong thing we do.* It has spoiled our world   *and us!* That s our human dilemma!

GOD IS DETERMINED to get his perfect world back, the Bible tells us, which is why Jesus Christ came to live in our world (there s historical evidence for that) to show us what a perfect life looks like. He laid down that perfect life when he died on the cross, on behalf of everyone who will ever trust and follow him, to cancel out the guilt of all the wrongs they ever do. God raised him from the dead (there s real evidence of that) to show that he was satisfied with all that Jesus Christ did, and now all who trust and follow Christ can be friends with God. *Then why, O why are people so content to live without God?*

GOD HAS SOLVED the human dilemma of everyone who trusts and follows Jesus, which is why *he* is such an essential Person to know about. Jesus said, I am the Way, the Truth and the Life (John 14:6). For 2000 years people all over the world have found those words to be true. If you want to know how true they are, then first you must under stand the damage that sin has done to you. That s the subject of the chapters that follow, based upon what the Bible teaches us; read on

John Appleby and Peter King
2004

Introduction

In order to answer the question why people are content to live without God, we need to examine what the Bible calls 'sin'.

We shall do that under five headings:

- What sin is (chapter 1)
- Why it is so wicked (chapter 2)
- How we may know that sin's nature is so wicked (chapter 3)
- Why it is so necessary to understand the real harmfulness of sin (chapter 4)
- What we can learn from all this (chapter 5)

Before looking in detail at these headings, we will remind ourselves of four basic facts explained in the Bible.

a. To begin with, we know that God originally made everything perfect and good. 'God saw all that he had made, and it was very good' (Genesis 1:31). Nothing of all the variety of things which were created at the dawn of history could find fault with its Maker, or complain of being defective in any way. So how has our present situation come about?

b. The Bible tells us, secondly, that the two most glorious of the creatures which God created, angels and human beings, lost their perfection. Some of the angels rebelled against God and were therefore thrown out of heaven (Jude 6). Persuaded by one of them (Satan), the first man Adam (who was the representative of all mankind) disobeyed God's clear command, and with his wife Eve was ejected from the Paradise in which they had been living (Genesis 3).

> Therefore, just as *sin* [i.e. disobeying God's instructions] entered the world through one man, and death through sin, and in this way death came to all men, because *all sinned*... [i.e. in their ancestor and representative, Adam] (Romans 5:12).

c. God punished the fallen angels permanently (Jude 6), but has shown great mercy toward mankind by sending his Son, Jesus Christ, into the world as the God-Man to be the Saviour of those who acknowledge their disobedience of God, by offering the perfection of his own obedience to his Father on their behalf. 'Christ Jesus came into the world to save sinners' (1 Timothy 1:15).

d. Finally, the fact that it was necessary for God to do this implies that we need someone to save us from our sinful disobedience of God; why else need Christ have come? So because we have disobeyed, we need to repent. Christ is God's appointed way of calling people to repent: 'I have not come to call the righteous, but sinners to repentance' (Luke 5:32). Therefore we need to have faith in Christ as our Saviour. The Bible insists that the Holy Spirit came into this world to give repentance and faith to the people. Why would he do this if we have no need of them?

In the light of these four basic Bible facts, we can begin to see how bad a thing sin really is, and the seriousness of the deadly effect that it has on our lives. Realising this helps us to see by contrast how wonderful the merciful grace of God is – that he should so love us as to want to redeem us. That in turn should draw us to exercise faith in Jesus Christ. We also understand how right and good God's laws – which we disobey – must be, for him to send his own Son as our Redeemer. Sin is an ugly disease in us, contrasting with the incomparable health and beauty of God's perfect holiness.

We cannot argue that God is not good when his laws condemn us as guilty and worthy of death because we disobey them. Both God and his laws are perfect and good, with no fault in either of them. God's good laws condemn us because of what we are – we bring condemnation on ourselves because we do not follow them. A condemned person standing in front of a judge may claim that it is cruel to condemn him, but the judge will justly say, 'No, you condemn yourself – you have broken the law!' If we do not disobey, we will not be condemned. 'We also know that law is made not for the righteous but for lawbreakers and rebels, the ungodly and sinful, the unholy and irreligious' (1 Timothy 1:9). It is the wrong the person did, their sin, which brings them into condemnation.

We can conclude with this summary;
- The law of God is good in every part. It is perfect and just, teaching us how we should live.

- When God's law is violated it justly condemns us as law-breakers and sinners.
- The law condemns both the person who sins and the sinful act, and the guilty can find no reason to blame it.
- We die because we break God's law – unless God's grace intervenes.
- God uses his good law to condemn the sinner. Yet sin, which causes the sinful act, afterwards condemns to death.
- The nature of sin is so deceitful that it uses a good law to bring a bad end, like turning food into poison.
- God's law shows sin to be vile and deadly – harmful to us.

We now continue to show what sin is – what it consists of.

1.
What is sin?

To sin is to break God's laws in our thoughts, words and actions. "Everyone who sins breaks the law; in fact, sin is lawlessness" (1 John 3:4).

God requires us to abstain from doing evil, and always to do good. When we do not obey, this is a sinful act. Whether we do many things wrong or only a few, each time we fail to satisfy God's requirement we sin. "For whoever keeps the whole law and yet stumbles at just one point is guilty of breaking all of it" (James 2:10).

There are no laws against what the Bible calls "The fruit of the Spirit" which is described as including: "love, joy, peace, patience, kindness, goodness, faithfulness, gentleness and self control" (Galatians 5:22-23). But there is a law against the works of the flesh.

We do not only sin when we do what is wrong. It is also sin to fail to do good.

With these thoughts in our mind we can proceed to chapter 2 "Why is sin such a wicked thing?"

2.
The sinfulness of sin

God's laws are holy and right, because he is holy and right. They are also for our benefit since we are creatures made by God. The wickedness of sin, therefore, arises from the fact that to break those laws is:

1) to act against God's wishes, *and*
2) to act against our own best interest.

When we do not keep God's laws we dishonour him and devalue ourselves. For those two reasons, we ought to hate such failure. By explaining the seriousness of both these consequences I hope now to show why offending against God by our disobedience is such a great evil. I hope the result will be that we shall hate sin as much as God does.

1. When we sin we act *against* God

The Bible says those who fail to keep God's laws are his enemies; hostile to God (Leviticus 26:21); rebelling against him (Isaiah 1:2); quarrelling with God (Isaiah 45:9); hating and fighting against him; blaspheming his name and even denying he exists. 'The fool says in his heart, "There is no God"' (Psalm 53:1). Merely to have an attitude of mind which gives no thought to God is described as actively hostile to him.

> The sinful mind is hostile to God. It does not submit to God's law, nor can it do so. Those controlled by the sinful nature cannot please God (Romans 8:7 8).

Let me illustrate further.

1.1 Sin is contrary to God's divine nature

All that God says and does is perfect because he is holy and cannot be otherwise, for perfection is an essential glory of God. There is therefore nothing more opposite to God than sin, for he cannot act against his own nature or he ceases to be God. 'Your eyes are too pure to look on evil; you cannot tolerate wrong' (Habakkuk 1:13) is how a prophet in the Old Testament speaks about God. Our failure to obey God's holy law which he designed for our benefit is so serious that God hates it. As there is no evil in the holiness of God there is no goodness in our sin. God is the perfection of all that is good; sin the imperfections he sees in us is the greatest of all defects.

1.2 Sin opposes the significance of God's names and characteristics

For example:

a. The sinful mind will not accept that God is King of kings and Lord of all lords. Pharaoh of Egypt, when Moses confronted him with Israel's God, said, 'Who is the LORD, that I should obey him? (Exodus 5:2) Thus the unbelieving mind will not accept God's sovereignty but seeks to dethrone him.

b. Valuing the enjoyments of this life more than seeking the spiritual benefits of a godly life implies that God is not sufficient. In effect, we say that it is better to be elsewhere, as the prodigal son did in Luke 15. A sinful attitude of unbelief says that God is not enough, denying the truth that he is sufficient.

c. Disobedience of God's good laws is a challenge to his *justice*. Justice and truth are part of his holy character, but when we deny his laws are right, by disobeying them, we also deny he is just and good.

> You have wearied the LORD with your words. How have we wearied him? you ask. By saying, All who do evil are good in the eyes of the LORD, and he is pleased with them or Where is the God of justice? (Malachi 2:17)

d. God is omniscient, that is, he knows everything. To suggest that he has no interest or knowledge is to deny that truth. He is the all knowing God, to whom all things are revealed (Hebrews 4:13).

e. God is rich and generous to all his creation, graciously providing every necessary blessing to make this world habitable. To dismiss this undeserved favour and goodness to us is to oppose him in unbelief.

f. To take the good things of this life which God gives and use them in ways that are contrary to God s wishes is to turn grace into evil practices. Sometimes people even suppose that if he is a gracious God, his grace will seem more wonderful because he allows us to sin so much! Such behaviour perverts the true meaning of God s *grace.*

These sinful ways challenge God s justice; abuse his mercy; take advantage of his patience; despise his power; make light of his love.

1.3 Sin is incompatible with what God does

Sin is incompatible with what God does for it is not just contrary to his nature, but also to his works. The Bible makes it clear that sin is actually the work of the devil who opposes God. He who does what is sinful is of the devil, because the devil has been sinning from the beginning (1 John 3:8). At the creation of the world all that God made was beautiful and good, but the disobedience of Adam and Eve introduced the rebellious influence of the devil into the world. As a result, the thinking and behaviour of those who neglect God has pene trated human society so that God s name and nature is con tinually forgotten in the world. From that neglect spring all the works of sin   disorder, confusion, ugliness, misrule, corrup tion, cruelty, disease and death   which trouble all of us.

1.4 Sin is disobeying God s law and neglecting his will

Sin is any expression of a person s will which seeks to oppose the worship of God in the world and which tries to separate us from God and what he requires of us, so that we cannot benefit from communion with him. The sinner shows hatred to God by opposition to prayer, preaching and holiness of a spiritual life. However, the Old Testament King David fulfilled God s will and is described as a man after God s own heart (1 Samuel 13:14).

1.5 Sin is contrary to the image of God

Adam and Eve were made perfect, in the likeness of God, but we are no longer like that. As darkness contrasts with light, hell with heaven, or ugliness with beauty, so disfigured are our sinful natures that they are now the opposite of God s holiness and rightness. The Bible teaches that the one who does what is sinful is of the devil (1 John 3:8).

1.6 Sin is contrary to the people of God

Christian believers have the comfort of peace with God through faith in Jesus Christ. Our sinful natures seek to hinder and even destroy that comfort. The closer we are to God, the more vehemently sin will try to break that relationship, for the sinful nature desires what is contrary to the Spirit, and the Spirit what is contrary to the sinful nature. They are in conflict with each other, so that you do not do what you want (Galatians 5:17) The devil hates everyone, but especially the children of God; yet he cannot hurt believers as much as God loves them, nor do them more harm than God can do them good.

1.7 The glory of God is the target sin seeks to destroy

We glorify God when we confess our sin, and repent of our wickedness, but sin tries to stop us. The sinful nature feeds the believer with false reports of God s nature, to inhibit the Christian who is living for God.

1.8 The very existence of God is questioned by sinful attitudes

People who are controlled by sinful thoughts hate God and seek to ignore or even destroy his existence. They try to shut out God from their thoughts and actions (Romans 1:18 32).

Before we go any further, let me ask you to pause and think over what has been said so far. I want you to listen to what God teaches in his Word, the Bible. How can you love such an ugly thing as sinfulness? Do you not wish to run away from it as from an enemy? Will you love what God hates, and hate what God, your maker, loves? No act or sinful thought can do you any good, but only harm and ruin. Do not argue with God, who is stronger than you are strong enough finally to turn the wicked into hell!

2. When we sin, we act against our own interests

2.1 Sin is contrary to what is physically good for us as human beings

This follows from the fact that we are made in the image of God (Genesis 1:26): whatever is evil in God s sight is therefore harmful to us. Our highest good is to be in perfect fellowship with him. The commandments, which God laid down for us to keep, were not simply to express his holy nature, but were for our benefit as his creatures. I want to show, in more detail, the ways in which sin is so harmful to us both in this life and the next.

a. Sin is harmful to our bodies in this life. At the creation Adam and Eve had perfect bodies which could not die, as long as they obeyed God's wishes. Death is a consequence of sin (Romans 5:12), and as soon as Adam and Eve sinned their bodies became subject to death. Now all people are destined to die (Hebrews 9:27). Our bodies are condemned to return to dust as a result of sin.

b. Sin is harmful to our souls in this life and the next. Harm to our souls is more serious than harm to our bodies. Our bodies live once and then die; our souls live forever. Jesus said,

> Do not be afraid of those who kill the body but cannot kill the soul. Rather be afraid of the One who can destroy both body and soul in hell (Matthew 10:28).

To suffer in our bodies is preferable to sinning against our souls!

Both these points can be explained in more detail, for they affect both our natural human life and our moral life. For example:

(i) At creation Adam and Eve were placed in a perfect environment. Everything there was for their physical health and enjoyment. But as soon as they sinned by disobedience God turned them out of that Paradise.

They lost all its benefits and became like pilgrims and beggars in a cursed world. They had to live by their own hands and earn their food by the sweat of their physical labour.

When the Lord Jesus came into the world to redeem sinful men and women, he had to come possessing nothing. He was Lord of all. Yet because he came in the likeness of our fallen humanity, he had to be a man of sorrows, destitute and homeless (Luke 9:58). That shows us that human beings have now lost the great inheritance of life in the Paradise into which our first parents were placed. Sin has robbed us of our natural inheritance.

(ii) Sin has robbed us of the natural rest and ease which we love so much. When we have finished our work there is little to show for it (Ecclesiastes 2:22 23). Life in Paradise was easy and pleasant but now it involves frustration, pain and sweat (Genesis 3:17 19).

(iii) Sin has robbed us of much comfort and joy. Our laughter can often turn to tears. In Paradise God s blessing made Adam and Eve rich and added no sorrow, but now our sweetmeats have sour sauces! For women the joy and wonder of childbirth is accompanied by discomfort and pain.

(iv) No one is immune from sickness and ill health. Before sin came into the world, there were no sicknesses. Even if we eat the best of foods, use the most effective medicines, and take the best care of our bodies, Each man s life is but a breath (Psalm 39:5). At our best we are brittle pieces of humanity, because the disease of sin works against our health.

(v) Sin troubles our natural consciences. When we are at ease all other troubles can be endured. A cheerful heart is good medicine, but a crushed spirit dries up the bones (Proverbs 17:22). So sin takes away the contentment of a good conscience.

(vi) Sin has deformed the perfection of our bodies. There was no such thing as deformity in the natural world at creation. God saw all that he had made, and it was very good (Genesis 1:31). But now we only become vain as we try in various ways to regain that lost beauty.

(vii) Sin has created disharmony between our bodies and our souls. Our physical feelings may lead us one way but our minds warn us against it and our wills are confused. At creation Adam and Eve knew what was right, loved what was right and did what was right, until they fell into the sin of disobedience. But now our souls are often prisoners to our physical senses.

(viii) Broken marriages and immoral behaviour are the result of sinful weaknesses in human nature. Sin has spoiled the health of society, breaking relationships in Church and State, creating divisions and factions, disharmony and mistrust.

(ix) Sin not only damages human well being, but often prevents our being at all! How many die in the womb, in childbirth, in infancy! Thousands die daily from sickness, and many more from war and natural disasters. Compared with the life span of those who lived in the beginning of world history, our life span is now reduced greatly. Someone who is born today is not sure to live a day.

All these points could be enlarged, but what is here is enough to show that sin is against the good of human beings in every natural aspect of this life.

2.2 Sinfulness has damaged the moral nature of human beings

God made us noble creatures, a little lower than the angels (Psalm 8:5). But sin has so spoiled the original excellence of mankind that now we are almost as low as devils.

a. This moral damage has affected all the physical faculties of our bodies. We can curse with our voices, deceive with our words, use our eyes lustfully, show pride in our faces, close our ears to what we should hear, do wicked things with our hands, walk into evil with our feet. Which of our physical faculties have we never used to commit sin?

b. This moral damage has also harmed our souls. At the creation human nature was righteous and holy like God. But Adam and Eve s sinning, by disobeying God s instructions, has robbed mankind of the privilege of displaying God s holy character. The original godly excellence has been lost, so that now it is no longer obvious that human beings were created by a holy God, and therefore belong to him.
Jesus himself explained that, Out of the heart come evil thoughts murder, adultery, sexual immorality, theft, false testimony, slander (Matthew 15:19) All these things bring moral defilement to our souls. And this damage to our souls means that men and women will not repent and listen to God s wise advice that we should turn back to him. Instead we stumble on in rebellion against him we will

not listen to the message you have spoken to us in the name of the LORD, as the people said to God s prophet Jeremiah.
 We will certainly do everything we said we would: We will burn incense to the Queen of heaven and will pour out drink offerings to her (Jeremiah 44:16 17).

c. This moral soul damage affects our understanding. It is by our understanding that we do things; so if our under standing is flawed we are unable to make wise judgements. That lack of wisdom leads to immorality and many other misdeeds. Our damaged understanding has made us what the Bible calls fools : we are wise to do evil, but not to do good which is illustrated by a number of facts:

(i) We behave as though we are groping in darkness. We struggle to find happiness and hope amid the troubles and trials of this life, grasping at ideas which prove to be shadows, in a vain attempt to find truth and reality. As Solomon, the wise man said,

> Of making many books there is no end, and much study wearies the body. Now all has been heard; here is the conclusion of the matter: fear God and keep his commandments, for this is the whole duty of man (Ecclesiastes 12:12 13).

(ii) Though the light of truth shines, because of our dam aged understanding we do not see it. The Lord Jesus Christ came to give us this light of truth, but until we are con verted we cannot see that he is the light of the world! At the creation, Adam and Eve could talk directly with God with understanding. But now the preaching of the truth of

God seems like foolishness to many because they cannot understand (1 Corinthians 2:14).

(iii) The fact that people so easily do so many wrong things is a further evidence that our understanding is damaged. It is the blind person who most easily falls into traps! If people could see the dangers which follow acts of sin, they would be less likely to commit them.

(iv) How common it is that people think they are going to heaven, but because of their damaged understanding they do not realise that it is hell towards which they journey! So many do not know what the end of their life will be.

(v) The teachings of Christ are not understood by unbelievers, because they are offended at him. The reason why they find fault with him is that his teachings find out their faults. If they knew Jesus they would never be offended with him.

(vi) We cannot see the future and do not know how best to prepare for the unknown. There is a proper time and procedure for every matter, though a man s misery weighs heavily upon him. Since no man knows the future, who can tell him what is to come? (Ecclesiastes 8:6 7)

(vii) Willingness to be led by others even by a dog is evidence of blindness of understanding. If a man was not blind he would scorn the use of a guide dog. How eagerly and how often we seek the advice of others. That in itself is an evidence of our lack of understanding of things and our awareness of the need for advice.

So sin has done damage to us, to our body s faculties and to our souls. It has so damaged our understanding that it has made us fools. And this folly is demonstrated in three great ways.

2.3 Our understanding of things has been distorted by sin

The Bible describes sin as folly; until a person fears God, they only play the fool. Take heed, you senseless ones among the people; you fools, when will you become wise? (Psalm 94:8) It is only when we see ourselves as God sees us that we understand the need to change our ways. The fear of the Lord is the beginning of knowledge, but fools despise wisdom (Proverbs 1:7). Such great foolishness is seen in three ways:

a. Our reason for living should be to enjoy God. Before sin came into the world, Adam and Eve enjoyed the happiness of knowing God. But since the coming of mankind's disobedience of God, we have become so foolish as to think that there is no happiness in knowing God, or even that there is no God.

Our foolishness is shown by the fact that we prefer to live for the comfort of our physical natures. But when all our efforts are for the benefit of our body we neglect our soul, which is the most important part of our human nature (Philippians 3:19). There are three things which prove that this life's pleasures are not the source of true happiness:

(i) Even in the garden of Eden, where everything was physically perfect, Adam's happiness was not just found in the things around him, but in God his Creator. What is only outside us cannot bring us inner peace.

(ii) Things inferior to us in their nature cannot bring us true happiness. Happiness comes from things we look up to and admire. God made the creation to serve us, not so that we should worship it. We are meant to worship him.

(iii) Nothing can give us greater love and happiness than the love of God himself. Nothing compares with God s love in sending his only Son to be our Saviour, to bring us the happiness of being reconciled to him!

b. We are ignorant of where happiness is to be found and how to gain it. Nothing is more knowable than that God exists (Romans 1:20) and yet he is so unknown (John 4:22; Acts 17:23). Sin has made us either worship a false God, or worship him in false ways!

> (i) To worship idols is foolish. Some worship idols they have made, and ignore the God who made them. Some people even worship the devil himself (2 Corinthians 4:4).
>
> (ii) Worship which is designed by ourselves, rather than being based on what God commands, is merely supersti tion. Such worship makes the *way* we worship more im portant than the *Person* we worship; it is not worshipping a false God, so much as worshipping God falsely. It is often motivated by fear and not love, and brings no true joy or comfort to the worshipper.

c. We foolishly ignore, or misuse, instructions which God has given us. The Bible tells us how God wants us to worship him. God has declared his mind to us by Jesus Christ.

> For the grace of God that brings salvation has appeared to all men. It teaches us to say 'No' to ungodliness and worldly passions, and to live self controlled, upright and godly lives (Titus 2:11-12).

How people pervert the gospel, making God's graciousness into an excuse to sin! The invitations God gives are carelessly rejected, and his wise words are seen as a threat to our desires rather than as expressions of his love. Although there may be an outward acceptance of God, people remain lovers of pleasure rather than lovers of God (2 Timothy 3:4). Let us consider some examples of human folly:

(i) We often act hastily without considering the consequences of our action. Animals act without considering consequences – but mankind is created as a higher creature. 'If only they were wise and would understand and discern what their end will be!' (Deuteronomy 32:29) But people often say, 'I never thought of this'. That is the language of fools. If we remembered that the wages of sin is death we would be more careful.

(ii) People often laugh at sin, enjoying it as a clever action. 'Although they know God's righteous decree, that those who do such things deserve death, they not only continue to do these very things but also approve of those who practise them' (Romans 1:32).

(iii) Some say that it is a waste of time to serve God. But when we come to the end of this life there will be a clear difference between those who have feared God and those who have not. Then it will be obvious that it has not been a waste of time to serve God (Malachi 3:14 18)!

(iv) We take good things from God and rarely say Thank you . Sometimes we even use his gifts to us in order to satisfy our selfish and unholy desires.

(How many meals are eaten and enjoyed without giving thanks to the God who originally provided the food? Editors)

(v) If God corrects us, or afflicts us by some painful provi dence, we sometimes get angry, and complain. Correction is not pleasant but we do need to be disciplined for our future good. What is more foolish than to speak against a good God?

(Venning follows with two points here which we have included under (v) as expansions of the same thought Editors)

Sin has made us so conceited that we are often unteachable. Some people, having once learned of and followed God s ways, have returned to the unbelieving ways of the world. One who does this is a double fool! Whoever, having been cured of a disease, would deliberately go and catch it again?

2.4 The effect of sin has so degraded us that we often act like animals

Our behaviour belies our true nature as made in the image of God.

(i) Sin has made mankind capable of behaving like beasts. There are several passages in the Bible where people are called brutish, e.g. Psalm 73:22. We can be like beasts in ignorance and stupidity, thinking more about our bodies than about our souls. Being sinfully brutish we cannot have fellowship with a holy God.

(ii) Those who live sinful lives can sometimes display *characteristics worse* than those of animals not the harmlessness of sheep and doves but the viciousness of wolves, lions and bears.

(iii) Sinfulness can make people *more beastly* than the worst animals. Animals keep the laws of their own natures. Ignorance is no crime in an animal, but it is in a human being. We can be more hurtful to one another than animals are to their own kind.

There are two animals which the Bible says are descriptive of people the sheep and the goat. Unbelievers are likened to goats; believers to sheep. The different natures of the two animals illustrate the different natures of believer and unbeliever. There is no doubt that the effects of sin can make us behave like animals.

2.5 Sin has separated men and women from God morally and spiritually

Sinners are described as far away from God (Ephesians 2:13).

(i) God is hidden from us. In the garden of Eden Adam and Eve could talk with God face to face. But after their sinful disobedience of God s command they hid from God. Even the believer who seeks God now has only an imperfect experience of God, by faith. Sin has damaged our ability to know God.

(ii) Sin has separated us not merely from fellowship with God, but also from enjoying the life of God. So poor is our life separated from God that the Bible describes us as dead (Eph esians 2:1).

(iii) Sinners are separated from actually receiving the love of God. Instead, God is angry with the wicked every day (Psalm 7:11). Whoever rejects the Son will not see life, for God s wrath remains on him (John 3:36).

(iv) The effect of sin is that it cuts sinners off from close contact with God. We are never out of his presence, but cannot have fellowship with him. There is reconciliation through faith in Jesus Christ, but outside of Christ sinful ness cuts a person off from friendship with God.

(v) Sinfulness makes us enemies to God. We cannot enjoy the rights and privileges from God which Adam and Eve first enjoyed. And unless we repent and acknowledge our sin we shall lose all privileges from him forever.

This separation from God brings very serious consequences:

a. God hides his face from us. As God s prophet said to his fellow countrymen your iniquities have separated you from your God; your sins have hidden his face from you (Isaiah 59:2).

b. God does not hear the prayers of unbelievers. He delights to hear the prayers of his people, but not the prayers of the wicked because they do not cry out to me from their hearts but wail upon their beds (Hosea 7:14).

c. Sinful people are without real strength. Our strength, as creatures, is to be joined with our Creator in happy union.

d. By sinning we become fearful of God and ashamed to approach him. A guilty conscience makes people afraid to come to God. Adam and Eve were not afraid of God s presence until they had sinned then they ran from him.

e. Sinfulness causes people to harden their hearts and resist when they feel God is speaking to them. All these things are miseries which spring from being separated from God.

3. Sin affects what happens to us when we die; its effects are everlasting

If sinfulness could only affect us in this life, which is for a brief time, it would not be so serious, but its effects are for ever. If the mercy of God does not intervene, then the unbeliever can only look forward to an ever living death, while the believer can anticipate an endless heavenly life.

We must not think that God is unjust in such arrange ments. He only punishes where there is sin; it is the sinner s own fault if God s punishment comes, because God has clearly told us how to live and serve him. All people have been brought under God s wrath against sin by their sinfulness, for all have sinned and come short of the glory of God. On the other hand, it is equally true that all who believe and trust in Jesus Christ will be saved (Mark 16:16).

We should understand that the anger of God in condemning sinners is the greatest punishment which can happen to a person. To be damned is misery, *altogether* misery and *always* misery. Nothing worse can ever happen to a person. We are told that Jesus will say to the wicked depart from me, you who are cursed, into the eternal fire prepared for the devil and his angels (Matthew 25:41).

From those words of Jesus we learn that at the last day the wicked will publicly hear their condemnation. Sin is *failing to do* what God says is good, and *doing* what he says is evil: so hell is a denial of what is good and the inflicting of what is evil upon the sinner. Hell is a real place, upon which God s curse rests, and an everlasting place. And the devil and his angels will be present there. Hell means that:

a. Those who remain outside of Christ s salvation will be deprived of all the good things of this life. The wicked are described as men of this world (Psalm 17:14). In other words, they have their benefits in this life. But they must part with this temporary happiness (Luke 16:25) if they leave this world as unbelievers. The unrepentant sinner goes from all the good of this life to all the evil of hell; but the believer goes from the evils of this life (and a little good) to all the good of heaven!

b. Sinners must part not merely with the good things of this life, but also part with the pleasure and delight they had in them. The rich man in Luke 12 did not cheer himself merely because he had many good things, but because he expected ease and joy from them. The songs of this world will no longer stir the heart with joy. Even the memory of such joys will bring no pleasure in hell.

c. There is no peace for the wicked in hell. There will be a clear understanding of God but no opportunity to repent.

d. In this life wicked people may possibly have a hope of heaven. But in the next life even that assumed hope will be gone. When a wicked man dies, his hope perishes; all he expected from his power comes to nothing (Proverbs 11:7).

e. There will not be one good person (i.e. true disciple of Christ) in hell. In this life such good people suffered the ridicule of the wicked; in the next life, the wicked would be glad to find just one good person!

f. No one can ever cross from hell to heaven. There will never be one wicked person in heaven, nor one righteous person in hell.

g. Those in hell suffer the loss of God himself. This means that they will have no mercy, no one to care for them, no future hope. Whom have I in heaven but you? (Psalm 73:25) was the cry of the Psalmist, as though nothing else mattered.

Hell is forever and so is heaven. Nothing is forever in this life, because here there is continual change. So,

> Whatever your hand finds to do, do it with all your might, for in the grave, where you are going, there is

neither working nor planning nor knowledge nor wisdom (Ecclesiastes 9:10).

There is no possibility of any change for the better in hell.

4. The damnation of hell is not a dream

I earnestly pray that none of my readers will come to such a place, but only hear about it, and that your hearing of it may be the means of your never feeling it. No eye has seen, nor ear has heard, no mind has conceived what God has prepared for those who love him (1 Corinthians 2:9). The same is true for those who hate God!

a. Even the ungodly use the term hell to speak of some intolerable misery. But all the miseries of this life are not to be compared with the misery of hell. Jesus said that to pluck out a right eye or cut off a right hand would be a pleasure compared to being punished in hell (Matthew 5:29 30).

b. Hell is as opposite to heaven as terror is to peace. Sinners go without the glorious life the saints obtain; Sinners are delivered to the misery from which saints are delivered.

c. Hell never ends. It is punishment without pity, misery without mercy, sorrow without succour, crying without comfort.

d. The Bible uses a number of pictures to describe hell. It is a place of sorrow, 2 Samuel 22:6; a place of pain more than any in this life, Psalm 116:3; a place of destruction,

Matthew 10:28; a state of fire, Matthew 5:22; a place of condemnation, Matthew 23:33; a place of torment, Luke 16:28. Hell is compared to a prison, Matthew 5:25; a bottomless pit, Revelation 9:11 (NKJV); a furnace of fire, Matthew 13:41 42; a burning lake, Revelation 21:8; outer darkness, Matthew 22:13, Jude 6 &13. Hell is a curse, a second death, a state of shame, Daniel 12:2.

e. There is nothing else in hell but great torment. It is universal torment there is no time without it, no part of the person can escape it, no cessation of it. I cannot go further without pleading with you, my reader: do you need anything more to dissuade you from going on in unbelief? Can you think calmly of going to such a place as hell? For your soul s sake hear, and fear, and seek Christ the Saviour of sinners!

f. Satan himself is the chief tormentor in hell. It is bad enough to be tormented by our fellow men and women what can it be like to be tormented by the devil himself?

g. The conscience of the wicked person will also torment them in hell. It may be possible to ignore one s conscience in this life, but in hell there are no pleasant things to divert attention away from the voice of conscience. Then the things which were deliberately ignored here will be un avoidable.

h. The wrath of God will also torment those in hell. Throughout this life God is very patient, letting many things pass apparently without comment. He is slow to be angry and has much mercy; but in the next life his patience is ended and his wrath is unleashed.

5. Are there greater punishments for some than for others?

a. Those who have lived long in sin, and die unrepentant will pay for their wickedness according to the time they disobeyed.

b. Those who have had more encouragement to repent and believe — those brought up in Christian homes, and Christian surroundings — are more guilty if they deliberately reject Christ. Remember the citizens of Capernaum, where Jesus taught and performed many miracles (Matthew 11:23).

c. Those who have understood God's law and the gospel message, and yet deliberately refuse to heed them will pay a greater price (James 4:17).

d. Hypocrites will know a worse hell. To appear pious and yet have no serious concern for God and his glory is a great sin.

e. Apostates will be treated as great traitors. These people are those who had followed the Lord but turned back and refused to repent. It would be better for such if they had never followed the Lord at all.

f. In short, hell means inexpressible sorrow, intolerable misery and persistent rebellion. They cursed the God of heaven because of their pains and their sores, but they refused to repent of their deeds (Revelation 16:11).

I have now dealt with the way sin is contrary to our good in this life, and in the life to come. I beg of you to think about what you have read, for if you repent of your sinfulness and believe God s message to us through Jesus Christ, then you will only know about hell by reading about it. There is only one result if you refuse to change your ways, for dying while still deliberately disobedient to God means hell is your end. I pass on now to bring evidence, in Section 3, that all I have said so far is true.

3.
Witnesses to the harmfulness of sin

1. God himself bears witness against sin

a. God does not leave us without clear instruction that wickedness is offensive to him. It is because God is concerned with our welfare that he has forbidden us to act sinfully. Instead he directs us to do what is good, just, honest and pure. God would not have forbidden sinful behaviour if it was acceptable to him and was for our good.

b. God does not even allow us to do the least evil that good may come to ourselves, or to others, or to the work of God.
 (i) We may not do evil to benefit ourselves. It is not wrong to be rich, but it is wrong to gain riches by sinning.
 (ii) It is wrong to tell a lie to benefit a friend. Paul was willing to die if thereby his countrymen could be saved, but not willing to lie for them (Romans 9:1 2).
 (iii) To think that we can benefit the work of God by some act of sin on our part is to make God dependent on the behaviour of the devil, who is the father of lies (John 8:44). Such sin is doubly repulsive to him.

c. God shows his anger at sin by threatening severe punishment against it. God said to Adam, you must not eat from the tree of knowledge of good and evil, for when you eat of it you will surely die (Genesis 2:17). If the sin of disobedi ence of God was not serious, would God have issued so severe a threat?

d. God is angry with the wicked every day (Psalm 7:11). Is sin not an evil thing and contrary to a good God if it makes him angry?

e. At the time of the flood it was the wickedness of people which made God so grieved that he had ever created mankind (Genesis 6:5 6). Such grief over his own creatures, who once gave him pleasure, is strong evidence of his displeasure at the wicked ungodliness into which they had fallen. If we do evil against God s commands he repents of the good he has done for us.

f. God has sent many severe punishments upon sinful people throughout history. Sinning cannot be insignificant if it brings such punishments upon wicked men and women. Adam and Eve were driven from Paradise for their sin of disobedience; Cain was punished for his murder of Abel; Ananias and Sapphira were punished for their lying to the early church (Genesis chapters 3 & 4; Acts 5:1 11). But not all of God s judgements follow the act of sin so immediately.

(i) We tend to think that God ignores sin because his judgements are not immediate. But if God were to bring judgements as fast as men and women sinned there would soon be no people left in the world! Yet ultimately their sin will be punished, even if it is not punished now.

(ii) Even God s people are punished if they commit sin, e.g. King David s adultery and act of murder cost him much sorrow and pain; Peter grieved deeply after his denial of knowing Jesus (2 Samuel chapters 11 & 12; Luke 22:54 62). Yet in the case of believers, forgiveness follows repentance for the wrong done.

(iii) God did not spare his own Son from punishment. Although he lived a sinless life, he took the place of all his believing people and suffered God s punishment due to them for their sinfulness.

2. Christ came into the world in order to condemn sin

a. Scripture makes it clear that Christ s sufferings were on behalf of sinners. God demonstrates his own love for us in this: while we were still sinners, Christ died for us (Ro mans 5:8).

(i) Christ s death is described as a ransom for sinners; it was the paying of a price. Christians are said to be bought with a price . You were redeemed with the precious blood of Christ (1 Peter 1:18 19).

(ii) Christ died as a sacrifice for sinners. Christ re deemed us from the curse of the law by becoming a curse for us (Galatians 3:13).

b. The seriousness of sin can surely be seen from the greatness of Christ s sufferings when he died for his peo ple s sake. He was described as a man of sorrows and familiar with suffering (Isaiah 53:3). We cannot really know the greatness of Christ s suffering because we have never known, as he did, God s unrestrained wrath upon us.

(i) He suffered *all kinds* of sufferings. No sooner was he born than suffering came upon him; he suffered opposition all his life; he suffered cruelly in his death. He suffered in his body in every part of his body. He was hungry, thirsty, weary, flogged, and crucified.

(ii) He suffered also in *his feelings*. No pity came from his enemies they just mocked him.

(iii) He suffered in his *soul*. When he was crucified he cried out, My God, my God, why have you forsaken me? (Matthew 27:46).

(iv) He suffered from all *kinds of people*. He went about doing good, yet the religious authorities plotted to kill him. He taught his own people, yet they turned their backs on him, and even his own family would not believe in him. One of his disciples betrayed him; another denied him. He continually did his Father s will, yet he was accused of serving Beelzebub (Matthew 12:24).

(v) All kinds of *humiliating circumstances* added to his suffering. He was equal with God, yet emptied himself and became a servant (Philippians 2: 6 7). He who cre ated a woman was born of a woman (Galatians 4:4). He who was sinless was made sin for us (2 Corinthians 5:21) and became a curse (Galatians 3:13). And there are many more ways in which he was caused to suffer, but I will pass on.

c. The greatness of all Christ s sufferings shows the sinful ness of sin. God could accept no way to satisfy his holy justice against sin except by the death of his holy Son. Surely this shows how much God hates sin and so we conclude the witness of God against sin, though much more could be said.

3. The angels bear witness against sin

a. Good angels. Scripture indicates that the holy angels in the presence of God in heaven hate sin (Jude 9). That which is food and drink to wicked people is poison to angels!

(i) Because they serve a holy God, angels will not sin. Indeed, they actively fight against it.

(ii) It was the angels who delivered God's law to the people of Israel (Galatians 3:19). The commands of that law are given to prevent sin by those who obey them.

(iii) Holy angels will not sin even to be revenged against the devil himself. Jude 9 describes how Michael the arch angel when disputing with the devil dare not slander the devil because to do so would have been sinful. We can easily repay evil with evil, but holy angels dare not sin that way.

(iv) There was an occasion when the apostle John bowed down to an angel. He immediately said, Do not do it! I am a fellow servant with you Worship God! (Revelation 19:10). The holy angels will not sin by stealing glory from God.

(v) The angels will rebuke sin even when they find God's people acting sinfully. Sarah, Abraham's wife, was rebuked for wrong actions (Genesis 18:12 15). When Zechariah would not believe the angel who promised him a son, he was struck dumb (Luke 1:13 20).

(vi) When an ungodly sinful person is converted, the angels sing for joy (Luke 15:7 10). When the wicked rejoice in their sins, angels grieve; when the wicked are converted from their sinful ways, angels sing!

(vii) God's angels oppose wicked angels and evil men. They protect Christian believers (Psalm 91:9 13), and serve their needs (Hebrews 1:14).

(viii) Angels carry out God s judgements upon wicked people. It was angels who brought destruction to Sodom and Gomorrah (Genesis 19:12 13) and at the end of the world it will be angels who sift the wicked from the true believers (Matthew 13:49 50).

I could give other examples of how the good angels witness against the evil of sin, but I will leave the matter here. But let us remember that the angels are present at our times of worship, and observe our behaviour (1 Corinthians 11:10). They are witnesses of all that we do, and in the final judge ment will be able to testify as to how we have behaved (Luke 12:8 9).

b. Wicked angels, that is the devil and the spirits that serve him, also show us how wicked sin really is.

(i) Even wicked angels believe there is a God, and they are frightened (James 2:19) because they know that God will punish them for their evil deeds. God did not spare angels when they sinned, but sent them to hell (2 Peter 2:4).

(ii) The devils know that God s judgement on them is just (Matthew 8:29) and thereby they confirm that sin is truly sinful.

(iii) They tempt people to sin. That which comes from the Evil One and his servants must be evil.

(iv) The devil disguises himself to look like a friend in order to try to deceive people. He paints sinful actions in attractive colours. If he had explained to Eve (Genesis 3:4 5) that he was an angel who had been banished from heaven by God, Eve would not have been tempted. But like an angler, he covered his hook with attractive bait!

(v) God permits suffering to come to us in order to teach us to be better children of his; but when the devil causes our suffering it is in order to make us sin against God. The devil's purpose in causing Job to suffer was not to make him good, but to cause him to curse God (Job 2:4 5).

(vi) When we come to realise that we have sinned, the devil adds to our distress by telling us there is no way out. He makes sin attractive before we commit it, but afterwards he makes us despair because of it. He tries to persuade people that the mercy of God and the merits of Christ are not enough to save them. This sin must be terrible indeed.

(vii) The devil is known as the accuser of believers. He accuses them before our God day and night (Revelation 12:10). He accused Job of only serving God because of the blessings God had given to him (Job 1:9 11). So he continually records the failings and the follies of believers. In that way also he confirms that the sins they have committed are an offence to God.

4. Believers give evidence that sin is evil

a. Christians witness against the sins of others. They try to prevent them. If that fails, they try to convince men of their sinfulness.

(i) Seeing the effects of sinful living upon others, believers will want to warn everyone about the consequences of wicked behaviour. I am about to go the way of all the earth, said King David to his son Solomon, so be strong, show yourself a man, and observe what the LORD your God requires (1 Kings 2:1 3). Similarly, Peter writes to early believers urging them to abstain from sinful desires (1 Peter 2:11).

(ii) If they find that their advice is ignored, believers will want to rebuke those who have ignored them. Old Testament prophets frequently rebuked their leaders for neglecting God s laws. John the Baptist rebuked King Herod for an unlawful marriage (Luke 3:19). The apostle Paul even rebuked the apostle Peter, who was acting in a way which denied fellowship to other believers (Galatians 2:11).

(iii) Wise people will grieve over the sins of others and separate themselves from their company. In so doing, the wise demonstrate that sinful living is evil. Wise believers will pray for those who commit sin and plead with God to pardon them, since such sinners will not do so for themselves. Abraham prayed for mercy for Sodom and Gomorrah (Genesis 18:23 32), Moses prayed for Israel when they sinned (Exodus 32:30 32), Stephen prayed for those who were stoning him to death (Acts 7:60).

b. Christians also grieve over and speak against their own sins. If they could avoid sin altogether they would, for they wish to live acceptably in God s sight. They do not only wish others to leave sinful ways, but wish to reform themselves also.

(i) They will not sin even when they have the opportunity. When Joseph in the Old Testament was tempted to sin by Potiphar s wife, he said, How then could I do such a wicked thing and sin against God? (Genesis 39:7 9) A right thinking person would rather suffer than commit sin.

Think of Daniel's three friends, who defied the king's command that they must not worship the true God and were prepared to be thrown into the fire (Daniel 3:18).

(ii) True Christians will not sin, even though they know they have God's gracious forgiveness through Christ (Romans 6:1 2). That forgiveness obliges them to avoid sin in every possible way. They must never do evil that good may come. Instead, they will take care to use every possible means to avoid sinning. They will fight against temptation, and will pray every day that they might be shielded from evil. They will get to know the Bible teaching so that when they are in a difficult situation they will know what to do as Christians. They will avoid any situation which might lead them to sin.

All these examples show that good people give evidence that sin is evil. But someone may argue that pious people only avoid sin because it upsets them, or is inconvenient, and not because they are concerned about God's glory. I can answer this false accusation in the following ways:

Firstly:
(i) The main reason why Christians seek to avoid sinning is because they know it opposes God's will. After his sin with Bathsheba, King David confessed to God, Against you, you only, have I sinned (Psalm 51:4). In fact, he had sinned against Bathsheba, against her husband Uriah, and against himself; but David's greatest concern was that he had sinned against God. For that reason Christians will condemn sin wherever it is found in others or in themselves. It is always against God.

(ii) Christians hate all kinds of sin. Their prayer is, let not one sin, from the greatest to the least, from the highest to the lowest, have power over me! They do not only detest open obvious sin, but secret and hidden sin as well. The human heart is such a maze of inner thoughts that we can scarcely grasp what secret sins hide there (Psalm 19:12).

(iii) Christians will want to avoid even the thought of sin. They do not merely pray that they may not actually sin, but rather that they may not even conceive the sinful thought (James 1:14 15).

(iv) The final proof that they oppose sin is that Christians do not only struggle to avoid it: they seek to do good. It is good to avoid doing wrong, but it is better to do good instead. The true believer will not only not commit evil but will also not omit to do good (Psalm 19:14).

Secondly, some may say, If godly people hate sin so much, why do they sin themselves? It is true that everyone is a sinner and does sin; to deny that would make God a liar when he says we are sinful (1 John 1:8 10). But I can answer:

(i) It is true that a believer may plan to commit sin; but more often they are led into sin unintentionally. They are led into sin by external temptation, not by inner choice. Sinning is against the wishes of their mind (Romans 7:23). For the most part, good people are captivated rather than active when they sin.

(ii) God does sometimes permit believers to fall into sin, in order that they may learn how unreliable and deceitful their hearts really are. Peter, the disciple, could not believe that he would ever desert his master and even deny knowing him. Yet when he was left to himself, that is what he did!

Yet in spite of the fact that believers can sin, I still say that godly people hate sin. This is shown by several facts:

(i) A godly person's conscience is greatly distressed when they realise that they have sinned against God (Psalm 73:21 22).
(ii) A Christian will be restless and oppressed by guilt until their sin is pardoned and cleansed from their minds. As King David once prayed: According to your great compassion, blot out my transgressions. Wash away all my iniquity and cleanse me from my sin (Psalm 51:1 2).
(iii) Believers will agree that God is just and right when he disciplines them for their sinful acts. Whoever says, God is right to chastise me for my sin, thereby condemns sin.
(iv) Peter wept bitterly when he realised how he had sinned by denying he ever knew Jesus, but afterwards he was far more eager and ready to serve Christ in any way he could. That repentance showed how he hated his sin.
(v) The believer's greatest wish is to be rid of sin altogether, but he knows that that is only possible when he is released by death to be with Christ. He will not wish to die for any other reason than that he will then sin no more. But he may well wish for this great change to come, as did the apostle Paul (2 Corinthians 5:4).

5. Even many unbelievers are ashamed of sinful behaviour

The ancient Greek philosophers, realising that a sinful life style degraded human beings. were agreed that such a life style was shameful. He who is wicked, said one of them, is the only miserable person .

Sinners are ashamed of sin *before* they commit it. This is evident because:

(i) they realise that their conscience will accuse them after they have sinned. They do not have the courage to stop and consider that, but rush to commit their sin. They will not carefully examine the consequences of what they propose to do.

(ii) If their sin had anything noble or honourable in it, why do they not loudly proclaim its virtues, and their own goodness in doing it? They do not do so because they are ashamed of it. It is vain for them to try to cover their sin by giving it a better name   calling drunkenness having a good time and immorality natural behaviour .

(iii) They seek to hide the shame of their sin by commit ting it in the dark (John 3:19 20). It is foolish of them to think their secret sins will be unknown (Ephesians 5:11 12*),* for darkness is no barrier to God. Thus they show that their wickedness is shameful by their efforts to keep it hidden.

(iv) There is no lasting pleasure for the sinner, either while they sin or afterwards, for their sense of shame and guilt is worse than their sinful desires. Even in laughter the heart may ache, and joy may end in grief (Proverbs 14:13). Sinful desires may be great, but the enjoyment of them will be little (2 Samuel 13:10 17).

(v) That sinners are ashamed of their sin is shown by the fact that they may seek to cover it under an appearance of godliness. King Herod pretended that he wished to wor ship the baby Jesus, but in fact he was determined to kill him (Matthew 2:8,16).

Sinners are ashamed of their sin *after* they have committed it. This is evident because:

(i) When they have done evil, they feel ashamed of it and are unwilling to own up to it. Instead, they make eager excuses for what they have done. If people do well, there is no need of excuses; if they do wrong, their excuses indicate that they are displeased with what they have done. Another way to cover their sin and hide their shame is to commit another one!

(ii) They may try to hide their own sins by severely criticising others who have done exactly the same wicked acts. In the Old Testament, Judah was guilty of incest, but he condemned Tamar his daughter in law for her immorality (Genesis 38). It is easy to see sin in others but to forget that we are sinners too.

(iii) Often when people realise they have sinned, they will carry out religious ceremonies in an effort to ease their sense of guilt. They will kiss a crucifix, pray through a rosary, go to confession, offer a sacrifice. To do so is an admission that they are ashamed of what they have done.

(iv) Even the wicked desire to go to heaven when they die; they have no desire to go to hell. Surely their actions cannot have been good if they are so unwilling to receive the inevitable wages of a wicked life everlasting separation from God and his heaven? The wages of sin is death (Romans 6:23).

It is true that many have a troubled conscience about their sin and its consequences. But there are also some who are happy to boast about their sinfulness. They are past shame, fear and sense. They glory in their wickedness. What can we say about their case?

Three times it is said of the shameless wicked in Romans chapter one, that God gave them over (vv 24,26,28). In other words, God allows them to sink deeper and deeper into wickedness until they are as consumed by it as the devil himself. To be wholly under the devil s domination is to be also under the devil s doom. Their boasting of sinfulness will not last!

In any case, do we ask blind men to judge colours? Or dead men to judge the affairs of the living? If men have so lost their sense and reason as to declare that snow is black and honey is bitter, do we believe them? So why do we take notice of the opinions of wicked people?

There are often special times when even hardened sinners will admit to shame for their actions. For example:

(i) When they come face to face with death, or incurable illness, their thoughts may change. The great King Nebu chadnezzar defied God when he was at the height of his power, but after a humiliating illness he admitted his wickedness and worshipped God (Daniel 4:33 37).
(ii) When the final great Judgement day dawns everyone will stand before God and accept his authority. The wicked will not be able to justify themselves, or be justified by anyone else. They will be speechless then.

(iii) Once they are experiencing the eternal state of separation from God and all goodness in hell, those who boasted of sin on earth will cry out at the devilishness of sin.

Thus it is clear that the wicked themselves show us the sinfulness of sin. And now I call another witness to this same truth.

6. All creation witnesses to the harmfulness of sin

a. The whole creation is not as it was when it first came from God s hand. Everything that God made was perfect; he called it very good . But how different things are now, since the power of sin came into the world through the disobedience of the first man and woman. The earth is under a curse (Genesis 3:17 19); the heavens are unclean in God s sight (Job 15:15); the best of humanity is vanity (Psalm *39:5);* the whole creation groans (Romans 8:21 22).

b. The animals God has made teach us our duty toward God. They all submit to his control, and do what he has designed them to do. Only the fallen angels and sinful men and women refuse to do what God has intended they should do. In this way they teach us:

(i) We should be dependent upon God, as they are. Jesus said,

> Do not worry about your life, what you will eat or drink... Look at the birds of the air your heavenly Father feeds them See how the lilies of the field

grow Your heavenly Father knows that you need [these things] (Matthew 6:25 34).

(ii) They teach us to be prayerful and trusting of God, as they are. It is God who provides for them by the resources of the natural world around them (Psalm 104:27; Psalm 147:9; Job 38:41).

(iii) They teach us to be fruitful and to fulfil the duties God requires of us. The earth drinks the rain and produces crops (Isaiah 55:10); the ox knows his owner (Isaiah 1:3); the flock feeds the shepherd (1 Corinthians 9:7). If our lives are barren and unfruitful, our gardens and fields will rebuke us; if we disobey God s wishes, our animals will rebuke us.

c. The creatures of the world around us show us our sins as well as teach us our duties. The ways in which we misuse many creatures demonstrate our sinfulness; Adam and Eve did not misuse the creatures of the garden of Eden. The clothes we wear tell us that sin has robbed us of the better robe of innocence that Adam and Eve wore (Genesis 2:25). Even the dust of the earth reminds us that since sin has so damaged us our physical bodies must return to dust (Genesis 3:19).

(i) The creation itself exposes as folly the idea of atheism. The very idea of creature supposes a Creator God. The fact that creatures exist supposes a First Cause and who is that but God? The fact of the existence of the creation leaves us without excuse if we do not believe there is a God (Job 12:7 11; Romans 1:19 20).

(ii) The creation witnesses against our sins of ingratitude.

The rivers flow continually, returning to the sea. In doing so they convict us of sin, for we so often make no grateful prayers to God, and even use his gifts to us for bad purposes.

(iii) The creatures teach us not to be idle. They are busy all their lives. Adam and Eve had tasks to do even in the garden of Eden. Human beings were not made to be idle. The apostle Paul said of idle people, that they should settle down and earn the bread they eat. Anyone who will not work should not eat (2 Thessalonians 3:10 12).

(iv) The lives of many animals are shaped by times and seasons of the year. They seem to be aware of the God ordered pattern of the seasons by which they regulate their lives. In this they are an example to us of how we should be alert to the purposes of God for us (Jeremiah 8:7).

(v) They make use of every opportunity which the natural world provides for their welfare, refusing nothing that is for their good. How unlike so many men and women, who know of God s gracious gift of salvation through Jesus Christ, and yet choose to reject it, though it would be for their eternal good!

d. God sometimes uses things he created for our benefit to punish us for our sinfulness. Water, which we need, was the means God used to punish the human race in the great Flood. Fire, which was given for our benefit, was used to burn Sodom and Gomorrah. The earth once opened and swallowed Korah and his family for the sin. Even the air we breathe carries diseases like the plague[1] (Genesis 7:17; 19:24; Numbers 16:31 32).

(i) In the normal course of events, rains help to bring about the fruitfulness of the earth. But sometimes, as a punishment for the sins of men and women, rains have failed and famine has resulted. God has used the failure of natural things as a means of punishment for sin.

(ii) Sometimes God has miraculously used natural things in ways that are contrary to their normal use, in order to demonstrate the wickedness of unjust and sinful attacks upon his own people, as when the water of the Red Sea divided to allow God s people to pass on dry ground (yet the same water returned to drown Pharaoh s army); and as the fire failed to even singe Daniel s three friends when they were thrown into Nebuchadnezzar s furnace. God miraculously altered the nature of fire to demonstrate the wicked injustice of Nebuchadnezzar s punishment of those godly men.

In all these ways. as I have shown, all creation declares the wickedness of sin.

---

[1] Venning s sermons were preached in London, and published as a book just after the terrible Great Bubonic Plague in England in 1669. In London alone 68,000 people died, and thousands more perished in other parts of the country. In late 1666 a great fire, which burned for four days, destroyed the old city of London. These events would have still been vividly in the memories of Venning s hearers at this point!

7. God's holy law condemns sin as harmful

a. Since God's law is holy and good, any action which breaks that law must be unholy and bad. God's law shows his authority as our Creator, and his goodness in providing us guiding principles for living. Any action which conflicts with his law must therefore be an attack on his authority and a denial of his goodness. Any transgression of God's law is therefore harmful and wrong it is sinful.

(i) God's law condemns sin before we commit it, forbidding all sinful acts. Instead, it describes what is good for us, what is our duty and what will bring us happiness. The law warns us, even before we sin, that anyone who does not do what is written in God's law is cursed (Galatians 3:10). Before it happens, we are warned that it is harmful!
(ii) God's law condemns our sinfulness *after* we have sinned. It makes clear the fact that, as sinners, we stand condemned by the holy justice of God. The righteous person has no need to fear God's law, but every broken law of God makes the law breaker guilty. When it has happened, the law shows us what harm we have done to ourselves.

b. The evil character of the power of sin is such that when it is forbidden it seems to gain more resolve to continue to offend. The apostle Paul explained, Sin, seizing the opportunity afforded by the commandment, produced in me every kind of covetous desire (Romans 7:8). When challenged by God's law, sin's reaction is to provoke us to sin more. We most want to do what we are forbidden to do!

(i) The Evil One actually used God s law to deceive Eve, by questioning what God had said about the trees in the garden of Eden (Genesis 3:1). Paul says that he was de ceived by Satan s use of the law (Romans 7:11). So Satan can deceive us by suggesting that we have not rightly understood what God has said.

(ii) The Evil One makes us believe that if we sin we shall not die, but live better. He told Eve that she would not die by disobedience, but be like God, being freed from the restrictions of remaining obedient. But Satan s real aim is to ruin men and women and so defeat God s good pur poses for them. Until Adam and Eve sinned, they were immortal; but once they had sinned they became mortal. The wages of sin is death.

c. God s law not only condemns sin, but also speaks clearly against the sinner. It does this in several ways:

(i) God s law cannot pardon even the least sinful act. We have only to break one command, and we are guilty of breaking all the commands by that disobedience. To break a necklace of pearls in one place is to break the whole, for one cut in the thread destroys the chain (James 2:10).

(ii) The law can never declare anyone Not guilty , be cause everyone has sinned. The presence of sin in us has made the law ineffective to justify us but strong to con demn us. The law cannot give us life, because the whole world is a prisoner of sin (Galatians 3:21 22).

(iii) The purpose of God s law is to awaken in the sinner s conscience the knowledge of what sin really is. The apos tle Paul tells us that he did not really know he was a covet ous person until he was convicted by the tenth command ment (Romans 7:7). The law shows us what an ugly, evil thing sinfulness is, and so speaks vigorously against it. For this reason the law of God is sometimes called a schoolmaster or guardian keeping us under its judgement unless and until Christ releases us (Galatians 4:1 5).

(iv) Some people may talk a lot about their good deeds; but when they are confronted by the law of God, they can have nothing to say in their defence, for all have broken the law. Such is the consequence of sin that silence has to be the only reaction from a sinner in God s presence (Romans 3:19).

(v) God s law, once broken, cannot be merciful; it can only condemn the law breaker. It cannot offer the sinner any hope, only judgement. There cannot be any doubt that the law of God is against sinfulness. But lest any should think that the message of the gospel of God s grace overlooks the severity of God s law, I must now explain how that gospel message also confirms the evil of sin, and the rightness of the law s severity.

8. The gospel message also bears witness against sin

Sinful behaviour finds no favour from the gospel message, which cannot overlook the smallest sin. The whole reason for the coming of Jesus Christ into the world was precisely to redeem men and women from sin. The teaching of Christ was that sinners should repent and believe in him. Both repentance and faith give witness against sin. Sin must be a great evil if sinners are to repent of it and turn from sinful living. Faith also denounces sin, because by faith we trust and obey God which is the opposite of sinning.

Every part of the gospel message speaks against the evil of sin. Those who believe that message are required to put off your old self, which is being corrupted by its deceitful desires; to be made new in the attitude of your minds; and to put on the new self, created to be like God in true right eousness (Ephesians 4:22 24). Such a complete change makes it clear that there is no way that the Christian can justify a sinful lifestyle. Yet, surprisingly, there are some who do try to use the gospel message as an excuse to justify sinning!

(i) Where sin increases, the grace of God can increase even more (Romans 5:20). So some are tempted to argue that if you sin, you cause grace to increase. To such an idea, the apostle Paul replied, By no means! We died to sin: how can we live in it any longer? (Romans 6:2) Jude argues that those so called Christians who feel that sinful acts can be justified are turning the grace of God into permission to commit wickedness and are, in fact, not Christian, but are ordained to condemnation (Jude 4).

(ii) The fact that Christ died for our sins is a glorious gospel truth. But some have argued that it allows us to sin, for Christ has died for us! Such a view misunderstands the gospel message, which is that Christ died to redeem us from all wickedness and to purify for himself a people that are his very own, eager to do what is good (Titus 2:14).

(iii) God has dignified believers with many titles of hon our, greater in significance than any earthly title held by great men and women. They are called children of God (1 John 3:1), a chosen people, a royal priesthood, a holy nation (1 Peter 2:9). If Christians have such nobility in God s sight, how can they justify living as disobedient sinners in his sight?

(iv) The day of judgement is yet to come, when all must give account of their lives. Because we know that, as Paul says, we try to persuade people not to sin but to live just and holy lives (2 Corinthians 5:11). So I have shown that the doctrines of the gospel message all testify that sinful behaviour is ungodly and wrong.

(v) All the exhortations and commands of the gospel message confirm the wickedness of sin. The gospel continually urges us to serve God in righteousness and holiness. This clearly shows us that sinful behaviour is displeasing to God and harmful to ourselves, and is to be shunned.

(vi) Many precious promises are made to believers in the gospel message. These promises are to draw us away from sinful ways of life so that we might escape the condemnation that sin brings. God s good promises are against the harmfulness of sin.

(vii) There are warnings included in the gospel message. God warns of judgement before we sin, in order that we may not commit it; he warns us of judgement when we have sinned, in order that we may repent. His warnings are obviously to draw us away from sin and lead us to repentance (Revelation 2:5,16, 22; 3:3, 19).

(viii) The experiences that we have of God s goodness and of our own deceitful hearts show us the harmfulness of sin. If God has been good to us, should we repay him by doing what displeases him? If we have learned that our deceitful hearts can mislead us, should we continue to trust them? Experiences of living the spiritual life confirm to Christians that to sin is foolish and dangerous.

9. Sin declares its own harmfulness and wickedness

This is the last of the various witnesses which I call in order to show the harm and evil of wickedness. And this I can demonstrate in several ways:

a. The names by which sin is described indicate the true nature of sin. For example, one name given to sinfulness is the work of the devil . If that is the case, then to sin is to be joined with the greatest of all sinners, for Satan was the first to oppose God, and will continue to oppose him till the end of time. And there are different ways in which men and women do Satan s work.

(i) To give in to temptation is to become a servant of Satan in that matter, allowing ourselves to be deceived about the teaching of Scripture; trying to tempt others to do what is contrary to God s commands; committing murder; spreading lies; seducing and deceiving others; falsely accusing others; hindering others from hearing and believing the gospel message; persecuting Christian believers these are all works of Satan, and to do any of them is to be a slave of Satan and to merit the same condemnation as him.

(ii) Satan knows that he cannot defeat the purposes of God. So he is happy to harm men and women as a means of gaining revenge against God. Such is his enmity to God that he will struggle to harm God s creatures. In so doing he himself shows that sin is harmful. In one sense, the sin of man is even worse than the devil s sin, because there is no hope for the devil. Demons do not sin against mercy and offers of grace, as men do.

b. Another name of sin is filthiness. Sinful living spoils both the body and soul of a person. The Bible uses words like loathsome, rottenness, corruption, disease, plague, gangrene, mire, dung all things which we take great pains to avoid in daily life. It is certainly a serious thing if dis eases infect our bodies; but it is a far more serious thing if our minds and spirits are so infected by sin that we happily serve Satan. Physical illness ceases at death; spiritual disease leads to eternal damnation.

(i) Sinfulness is everywhere in our world, and affects every part of our human nature (Romans 5:12; 2 Corin thians 7:1).

(ii) Sinfulness grows at an alarming rate; from the first sin of disobedience in the garden of Eden, it has now invaded the whole of humanity, and every part of human nature. It grows in human experience a lustful look can lead to immorality and adultery, which can then lead to murder! Sinful behaviour is seriously infectious, for one sinner can be copied in his behaviour by many other people (James 3:5 6).

(iii) The infection of sin is almost incurable (Jeremiah 17:9). God has punished sin in different natural ways, but none was successful except the final coming of his Son Jesus Christ to live a perfect life and die an atoning death on the cross as the supreme sacrifice for the sins of his people.

(iv) Sin even lives on in its effects after we are dead. Our bodies continue to corrupt and rot away in the grave, returning to the dust from which the human body was first made. The body of Jesus Christ did not corrupt in the tomb, for there was no sin in him.

So we have seen some of the names of sin and how those very names indicate its harmful nature.

c. Another evidence of the sinfulness of sin is the way in which it hides its true character in order to deceive us. Truth is never ashamed of openness, but sin, on the other hand, cheats and lies in order to hide its true nature. If sin could not harm us, why would it need to deceive us? Its deceptive behaviour declares its own sinfulness. For example:

(i) Sometimes Satan deceives us by declaring that a certain thing is not in fact sinful. Eve looked at the forbidden fruit and desired to have it. Satan assured her that it would make Adam and herself like God. He wickedly suggested that that was why God had forbidden them to take it (Genesis 3:5).

(ii) Some may justify stealing because they have no means to buy. We might forgive them because of their plight, but it remains a sin to steal.

(iii) Some may think that it is acceptable to sin just once . But that one sin will surely lead to another and then another!

(iv) People excuse their sin by claiming it was only a little one. But if the wages of sin is death, how can there be little ones?

(v) A sin committed in secret seems less sinful than a public act of wickedness. But since God sees all things, how can any sin be secret? (Psalm 139:11 12).

(vi) It may sometimes seem that an act of wickedness is the way to obtain some gain. But sin s gain is loss, for Jesus said that to gain the whole world by sinful means is to lose one s own soul.

(vii) We may think, others do it, why not I ? But tell me, what comfort will it be to have companions in hell?

(viii) It is true that God will forgive you if you sin and then repent, but he who promises forgiveness to those who repent does not promise repentance to those who sin.

(ix) Some say, But nothing has happened to you yet, despite your sinning . But not to be punished (when punishment might bring you to repentance) may be the worst possible punishment (Isaiah 1:15).

(x) Since you are a sinner by nature, how can you not sin? You do wicked things because of your sinfulness   what else could you do?

These are all ways in which sin seeks to excuse itself, and deceive you. And all those devices are evidences of the evil nature of sinfulness. It is impossible to speak worse of sin than it really is, or even as badly of it as it deserves   for it is the height of evil. It is not merely ugly, but ugliness itself; not only filthy but the essence of filthiness; not only abominable but the source of all abomination.

Now, in the next chapter, I must proceed to show you the usefulness of having learned the true nature of sin.

4.
The usefulness of understanding the nature of sin

1. There is nothing worse than sin

Nothing is more harmful to us than sin. The evil of sin is worse than trouble and distress, worse than death, worse than the devil himself, worse than hell. Those four things are truly terrible: we pray to be delivered from them. Yet not even all of them together are as harmful to us as a sinful life style. Let me explain:

Firstly, there are many troubles and distresses in this life. Is wickedness worse than them all? Yes, very much so! Jesus said, Do not be afraid of those who kill the body but cannot kill the soul. Rather be afraid of the one who can destroy both soul and body in hell (Matthew 10:28). In other words, it is better to be killed than to be damned. One may suffer and not sin; but it is impossible to sin and not suffer.

(i) It may be good for us to choose suffering: it is never good to choose sin. Three young men chose to suffer in a fire rather than to sin by disobeying God (Daniel 3). Moses chose rather to be ill treated with the people of God than to enjoy the pleasures of sin for a short time (Hebrews 11:25). It cannot be said that sufferings have no good in them. The Psalmist knew that it was good that he suffered (Psalm 119:71), but we can never say   It was good that I sinned. Wickedness is never good, either before or after it is done.

(ii) We should rejoice if we have to suffer, for troubles can keep the believer close to God whereas sin separates us from God. The apostle James wrote, Consider it pure joy, my brothers, whenever you face trials of many kinds because you know that the testing of your faith develops perseverance (James 1:1 2). We say that God takes pleasure in seeing his people tested by trouble because he knows they will become stronger Christians because of it (Romans 5:3).

(iii) The Bible contains many statements to encourage those who are suffering some trial, but never encourages anyone to act sinfully. God promises to help us when we are in the middle of troubles. But if we act wickedly, God withdraws his presence from us. To know God s comfort in our troubles is an evidence of his love for us because we are his children. But to enjoy a sinful lifestyle is evidence that we are not his children.

(iv) God can use troubles and trials to kill sinful desires in his children. The Psalmist said, before I was afflicted I went astray, but now I obey your word (Psalm 119:67). Evidently it was his troubles which caused him to turn to God. So to suffer some trial is better than committing sin, which can only separate us from God. God has a good purpose in sometimes permitting his people to suffer. But wickedness never has any good purpose. Sin never does any good. We have to say that sufferings can make believers more perfect, whereas sinning makes us more imperfect. Every ungodly sinner is without God and without hope (Ephesians 2:12), but a suffering Christian has both God and hope in his or her affliction!

(v) To endure persecution and suffering for Christ's sake, for God's sake or for righteousness' sake makes them glorious. To fight against sinful temptation and to avoid falling prey to it, even if we suffer as a consequence, reveals the beauty of God's power working in us. Better to be a happy martyr than to be a slave of evil, condemned by God's holy justice (1 Peter 4:1-16). Better to suffer than to sin!

Secondly, the evil of sin is worse than death. Death is a great enemy, as is obvious from people's reluctance to die. But sinfulness is an even greater enemy than death, as I can show;

Death means separation between soul and body, between loved ones, and from possessions; however it cannot separate believers from the everlasting love of God which they enjoyed while they lived. Wickedness is worse than death because it separates sinners from God's loving kindness while they live. Sin is worse than death because it was the first sin of disobedience (Genesis 3:6,19) which brought death into the world sin entered the world through one man, and death through sin (Romans 5:12).

(i) There is a fear in death. People are not only unwilling to die, but also afraid. Sin is the sting of death (1 Corinthians 15.56), because it brings to the sinner the everlasting hurt of separation from God. If sin had never come into the world, there would be no death (or certainly no terror in death). If the sting is taken out by faith in the death of Christ, there is no danger or cause of fear in death.

Since the children have flesh and blood, he too (i.e. Jesus Christ) shared in their humanity so that by his death he might destroy him who holds the power of death that is, the devil and free those who are all their lives were held in slavery by their fear of death (Hebrews 2:14 15).

(ii) Death deprives us of our natural earthly life. But sin deprives us of spiritual life now and eternal life in heaven. Death kills only the body, but sin confines the soul in hell. So we can say that evil kills more than death kills (Luke 12:5). Similarly, while death corrupts our body, sin corrupts the more important part of our human nature our soul. Indeed, it is not wrong to say that wickedness corrupts both body and soul, since sinful behaviour often affects the health of our bodies, as well as corrupting our souls. The consequences of a life of sin are worse than death. Jesus told his hearers that their greatest misery was not death, but to die as unforgiven sinners (John 8:21).

Thirdly, the evil of sin is worse than the devil himself, for it was sinful behaviour which made the devil what he is. The devil was not created by God as an evil angel. It was the devil s sin of rebellion against his Creator God which made him as wicked as he is (Jude 6; 2 Peter 2:4). Yet, when we sin, we are worse than the devil.

(i) The devil will tempt us, but temptation is not sin. The evil of being a sinner comes to us only if we commit the wickedness of obeying that temptation. The devil may tempt us to behave wickedly, but he cannot force us to do so. It is the sinful inclinations of our hearts which cause us to sin (James 1:14). Those sinful inclinations are present even in the believer whether Satan tempts us or not. The great early Church Father, Augustine of Hippo (AD 354 430), used to pray Free me from the evil man that is myself. No one, not even the devil himself, is as harmful to us as our own sinful inclinations.

(ii) Satan may tempt us and even torment us. The Bible describes him as a roaring lion (1 Peter 5:8); but even when he tempts and torments us severely, he does so from outside us. He does not live in our spirits, but our own sinful inclinations are *within* us. They are what prompt us to sin. That sinfulness is therefore worse than the devil himself.

Fourthly, even in hell the unforgiven sinner s own con science will torment him more than the devil, for the sinner cannot doubt that it is his or her own fault which has brought them to that place. Their own conscience will accuse and torment them. Sin has proved worse than any troubles or death or Satan or Hell.

We should consider well what an incalculable benefit it is when God pardons a sinner for Christ s sake, and redeems him or her from all these consequences of sin!

I have now shown that sin is more evil, more harmful to us than anything else. Let me emphasise this a little more:

(i) There is more harm in wickedness than there is good in all the benefit we have from the natural world. When we are ill, there are many medicines available to us in nature around us which can comfort and cure us, but nothing in this world can cure the disease of sin. Only God with his gracious pardon has the answer. Even perfect angels cannot help us: only God himself can remake us, by what the Bible calls a new creation (Ephesians 4:24). This is why King David prayed, create in me a pure heart (Psalm 51:10).

(ii) Wickedness is the only wrong thing that *must* be repented of. We may sigh, groan or sorrow over other wrong things, but God requires there to be repentance for wickedness. That is, the sin, the shame of it, and the evil consequences of it, must he confessed to God. Restoration must be made if we have harmed others, and we must avoid doing such a thing again. Repentance is a severe thing, full of rebuke and disgrace. That very severity is another evidence of the greatness of the evil which is in sin.

(iii) Continuing in sin is the only thing that can bring a person to the condition of being given over by God, as is said three times in Romans chapter 1 (vv.24, 26, 28). In other words, continual sinful rejection of what God re quires of us can actually bring a person to become irre deemable. Such is the greatness of the evil of sin.

(iv) The Bible tells us that sinfulness makes God hate wicked people (Psalm 5:5; Proverbs 6:16 19). Although his nature is love, such is the evil of sin that it has caused hatred in God himself. Can there be greater evidence of the wickedness of sin than this?

(v) Jesus Christ, who was uniquely God and man in one person, is the best and greatest Saviour. Therefore the salvation he gives is the best and greatest salvation. Sin must be the worst of all evils if it requires the best Saviour to redeem a sinner.

So I hope you will agree that I have shown how sinfulness is the worst of all evils, with which nothing else can compare. Now, in the next section, I want to spend some time to consider what this fact tells us about God, and what it tells us about ourselves.

2. We learn of the wonder of God's patience

If sin is so evil and contrary to God, then surely his patience is very great and his long suffering most remarkable. That God should plead with offensive sinners, his enemies, to be reconciled to him (2 Corinthians 5:20) is not like human behaviour it is the behaviour of a wonderfully patient God. It is a miracle of patience that he has shown his love through the life and death of his Son for sinners, and still calls and waits for them to repent despite the fact that they reject him and his love! Because of the LORD's great love we are not consumed (Lamentations 3:22).

(i) Think of the number of sinners that there are in the world. If there were only a few wicked people in the world, we might understand how God could be so patient and long suffering to them. But the whole world is under the control of the wicked one (1 John 5:19). There is not a person to be found who does not sin and has not sinned. How remarkable then is this patience of God!
(ii) If each person on earth had sinned only once, we could understand that the matter might not be too serious. Yet we all do things which are displeasing in God's sight many times each day. And this has been going on since the beginning of time since the first man and woman dis

obeyed the command of their Creator. Surely that makes God s long suffering miraculous!

(iii) There is a sense in which our sins cry out to God against us (Genesis 4:10). The devil, our adversary, is eager to make much of our wrong doings. Yet God seems reluctant to destroy us for our wickedness and still stretches out his hands in compassion to us, warning us of the danger of eternal punishment for continual rebellion against him.

(iv) Our sinfulness is made worse by the fact that we continue to do wrong despite God s continual goodness to us (Romans 2:4). We make vows and resolutions and then fail to keep them. When we are ill, we promise to be different when health returns but fail to change when we are well. In these ways we not only do wicked things but also aggravate the wickedness of them because we know we should do better. Yet God still waits to be gracious! Thus we learn that the great evil of sin magnifies the great wonder of God s grace in his being so long suffering.

3. We learn that God s punishments for sin are justified

God is far more patient than we might think, for sometimes he seems to overlook sinful actions yet sometimes he does clearly punish some of those who behave sinfully and do not repent. Eventually, all who fail to confess their sin will be eternally punished. So God often punishes less than the sin deserved, but never more so.

(i) Think about who God is! He is and cannot be other

than just in all he does.

Will not the Judge of all the earth do right? (Genesis 18:25) Cain complained that his punishment was more than he could bear (Genesis 4:13), but he had to accept that he deserved it. Eve complained of the devil (Genesis 3:13). The devil certainly can tempt us, but he cannot *compel* us to behave sinfully. We cannot prevent ourselves being tempted, but we can refrain from sinning. Nor can we complain against God (Genesis 3:12). God placed the first man and woman to live in the most favourable conditions possible! Did not God warn him of what he should not do and explain to him the consequences if he disobeyed (Genesis 2:17)? God has made clear to us in the Bible how we should behave. How then can we complain to him if our misbehaviour is punished?

(ii) Think about what sin is. The nature of evil and sin is to oppose God. So it becomes just for God to do to sinners what they would wish, unjustly, to do to him.

> I the LORD search the heart and examine the mind, to reward a man according to his conduct, according to what his deeds deserve (Jeremiah 17:10).

(iii) Think about the situation unbelievers are in. To die without repenting of our sins means that we are condemned to an everlasting sinfulness. Is it unreasonable that being everlastingly sinful should be everlastingly punished? If someone pays the debt they owe to God for their disobedience of his commands, then they can go free. But if that person says he or she cannot pay their debt, they must understand that they have made their own misery, because they chose to be disobedient to God. Such a person cannot plead for forgiveness for Christ s sake, for Christ did not die on behalf of the finally impenitent, but only for those who come repentantly to him for mercy. We can only blame ourselves if we refuse God s grace in Christ. God is not unjust to punish those who reject his mercy, but he is pleased to be merciful to those who seek him.

4. How precious is the forgiveness of our sin!

It is a great wonder that anyone is pardoned for their sin, seeing how offensive and rebellious sin is against God. The preciousness of this mercy can be seen in various ways:

(i) The mercy of pardon for sin is a gift of the New Covenant. In the Old Testament we read how God made an agreement with the nation of Israel to bless them if they obeyed his commands. It was a covenant based on their works. But because of the merit of the life and death of Christ, God has made a New Covenant with all those who have faith in Christ for their salvation. This New Covenant is called a superior covenant because it brings better blessings to believers by giving them free pardon for Christ s sake as an act of God s grace (Hebrews 8:6 12). It is a gift to believers on the ground of Christ s work, not of their works. Christ lived a life of perfect obedience to his Father s will and gave up that perfect life by his death on the cross as a complete sacrifice for the sins of all who trust in him (I Peter 1:18 19).

(ii) This forgiveness brings comfort and rest to the believer s soul. Anyone who is convicted of the guilt of their sinful behaviour will have little rest in their soul. They will always fear God's anger. But if that person realises that pardon is available by faith in Jesus Christ, then they can be at peace with God (Romans 5:1). The knowledge of sin makes us sick, but the knowledge of pardon makes us well. Surely we must say that it is a wonderful thing that God should pardon anyone's wickedness, seeing how offensive it is to the holy perfection of God and how harmful to us. God does for us what we cannot do for ourselves, or even expect that God should do for us! And this at the cost of the death of his Son! No wonder the prophet exclaimed, 'Who is a God like you, who pardons sin and forgives the transgression of the remnant of his inheritance? You do not stay angry for ever but delight to show mercy' (Micah 7:18).

Now that we understand how great the evil of sin is, we must say that no sinful act should ever be committed. It is against the will of God, against the purity, authority and holiness of God, and harmful to ourselves. No matter how much we may gain from some sinful act, or how much temporary pleasure it may give us, it cannot be justified, because it is against God, our Maker and heavenly Father. We should not even debate whether or not we may do something which we know to be wicked. There are two great wonders. One is that God should be so good to us, who are evil and do evil against him. The other is that we should do evil against so good a God. There is nothing so beautiful to the eye of God as holy living, and nothing so beneficial to us. How then can we carelessly commit sin?

5.
Things we can learn from the fact that sin is our enemy

To begin with, we must say that we are greatly deceived if we think that sinful behaviour is a way to happiness. Some have called evil good (Isaiah 5:20). It may seem that forbidden things are sweet, but after we have swallowed them there is a bitterness. Satan promised Adam and Eve that if they disobeyed God they would become like him (Genesis 3:5). But the consequence of their disobedience was very different indeed! As sin is, so are its effects wholly evil.

a. Sin can never be profitable for us. Sinful behaviour costs dear and profits us nothing. What did Cain profit by killing Abel (Genesis 4:13)? What profit did Judas receive for betraying Christ (Acts 1:18)? If it is argued that these are great sins indeed, what of little sins such as covetousness and lust? People commonly want more and more things — is that unprofitable? Yes! Consider the following:

(i) One wise man has said,

> I have seen a grievous evil under the sun: wealth hoarded to the harm of its owner, or wealth lost through some misfortune, so that when he has a son there is nothing left for him (Ecclesiastes 5:13 14).

Where is the profit in that hoarding?

(ii) No matter how much we have, and how much we use what we have, it will never wholly satisfy. The love of money grows faster than the money (Ecclesiastes 5:10 11). If material things cannot even satisfy our senses, how can they profit our souls? The labour of getting such things, the cares of keeping them, the fears of losing them, eat away at the comfort of having them.

(iii) We cannot take our possessions with us when we die; where then is the profit? Even if you say that the previous arguments I have used do not apply to you, without doubt this one does. If your life has been a gathering of posses sions because of a covetous spirit, then that sinful spirit has brought you no profit in the moment of death.

So we see that no profit comes by sinning, not even by covetousness, which is called the most profitable sin. The question is often asked, What profit is there in godliness? I answer, Godliness is profitable at all times, for here and for hereafter, for this life and for that which is to come .

b. Sinful behaviour can never be honourable. That which is a disgrace to the life of the soul can never be an honour to the body. That which is dishonourable to God can never be honourable to people. Even if all the world should admire some sinful act, God judges it vile. And he is doubtless the best judge of what is honourable.

c. There is no lasting pleasure in sin, only a temporary satisfaction. Even those who have lived in pleasure for many years are eventually overtaken by the infirmities of old age. Pleasure is the contentment of a person's mind in what they do or have. There is no such pleasure to be derived from wickedness by those who live in sinful ways. Consider these reasons:

(i) There is no peace for the wicked (Isaiah 57:21). Those who adopt a sinful life style may laugh and seem happy, but God knows that there is no peace in their hearts.

(ii) Sinning is not how human beings were meant to live, for mankind was created perfect in the image of God. Godliness should be our normal possession. So those who practise ungodliness are said to be dead while they live (1 Timothy 5:6).

(iii) Sinful behaviour can never fully satisfy human desires. To attempt to find contentment by ungodliness is like seeking to quench thirst by drinking salt water it only increases the thirst! It is pure water that quenches thirst.

Yet despite these reasons to the contrary men and women are still unwilling to believe that there is no pleasure from sinfulness. They are reluctant to believe that disobedience of God brings unhappiness unlike Moses, who knew there was no better thing than to serve God (Hebrews 11:25 26).

In any case, if there is any pleasure in a thing, it can only be to the physical and sensual part of a person. That part of us is only the shell in which the undying soul lives. It is that soul which is the glory of a human person, making them different from the animal creation. The soul can be affected by the pleasures of the body, but it cannot live on them. The soul is spirit and must have a diet that is proper for a spirit, that is a spiritual diet. We must conclude that there is no worthwhile profit, honour or pleasure to be had by sinful acts. Evil behaviour can only bring disappointment and sorrow.

There are still some further things we can learn from the fact that sin is our enemy, and I shall comment briefly on them now.

d. Time spent in sin is worse than time lost! Time spent in sinful ways has to be accounted for, and who can justify evil doing? What we sow in the seed time of this life we shall reap in the harvest of the next (Galatians 6:8). Time that is not spent in living for God is mis spent and worse than simply lost. Be very careful, then, how you live not as unwise but as wise, making the most of every opportunity, because the days are evil. Therefore do not be foolish, but understand what the Lord s will is (Ephesians 5:15 17).

e. To make fun of sin is foolish. There are many too many who sorrow when trouble comes, yet laugh over their sinful ways. Can it be wise to laugh at that which wearies God? There are many who laugh at the concept of hell; can there be anything more foolish than to laugh at that which destroys our life?

f. The harmfulness of sinful living teaches us that we should seek godliness without delay. It may prevent a good deal of ungodly living if, early in life, we seek to know God and his ways. How careful we should be to keep ourselves from everything which will keep us from happiness. God has promised that if we seek him we shall find him (Proverbs 8:17 21). The Bible gives us many good examples of young people whom God honoured because they honoured him in their youth Joseph, Samuel, Josiah, Daniel, the apostle John, Timothy.

g. Since sinfulness is so evil and harmful, how welcome the message of salvation should be to us! When we are unwell, the doctor and his medical treatment are so important to us. We even welcome surgeons, though their treatment may cause us pain. So dear is good health to us that we welcome these people s treatments, and even reward them for it! How we should welcome, then, the message of Jesus Christ, who comes not merely for the benefit of our temporal bodies but for the salvation of our eternal souls! To procure that salvation cost Christ dearly, but he gives it freely to those who will trust and follow him.

Advice to those who are not yet Christians

When the Apostles preached, those hearers who were not believers were sometimes so affected by the message that they asked, What must we do? If anything you have read so far has made you think about your own relationship with God, let me offer you some words of advice.

1. As Jesus himself said, Repent and believe the good news! (Mark 1:15)

a. To repent is to hate your sins, and yourself for committing them. Let it grieve you that God is displeased with your sinful living. Make it your whole aim to refuse to commit sin. To be merciful to sin is to be cruel to yourself Therefore do not spare acts of ungodliness, but abhor them. Let it be clear by your changed behaviour that you are a new person.

(i) Repent, then, and turn to God, so that your sins may he wiped out (Acts 3:19) was the message of the apostles. Forgiveness follows repentance that is the good news of the Christian faith.
(ii) Whoever truly repents says, in effect, If I had my life again I would obey God every day, as I intend to do from now on .
(iii) For some one to repent is such a wonderful thing that

it brings joy to all whom you have grieved by your sin to God, to the angels, to other believers.

(iv) But if there is no repentance, that person must face God alone, in the Day of Judgement. There will be no opportunity to repent then. God has given us time to repent now. There is no other opportunity than the present (Isaiah 55:6).

b. It is not only repentance that is required, but also faith in our Lord Jesus Christ. Repentance is not enough to make us perfectly right in God s sight; we need the perfection of Jesus Christ to be given to us. We have this by depending entirely by faith upon him for our hope of acceptance by God. We cannot negotiate with God for our salvation, by offering some kind of payment. As the Apostle Peter said about Jesus Christ, Salvation is found in no one else, for there is no other name under heaven given to men by which we must be saved (Acts 4:12). Even if you repent and then lead as good a life as you can, without faith in Christ you will not be good enough for God.

c. Do not return to your former sinful ways of life, having once repented of them. A dog returns to its vomit and a sow that is washed goes back to her wallowing in the mud (2 Peter 2:22). It will be difficult to repent a second time if, having once done so, people go back again into sin (Hebrews 6:6).

d. Take heed that you do not retain and continue to practise one particular sin. If once we have realised that it is the sinfulness of our lives which cost the Lord Jesus Christ his life blood, how can we continue even in one of them, whether in thought or word or deed?

2. Beware of sinful thoughts

We can hide our thoughts from our friends, but not from God, for he reads our hearts. It is easy to appear holy while plotting evil in our hearts. It is possible to think sinfully while not committing outward sin (Matthew 5:21 22,27 28). To enjoy the memory of past sinful behaviour is to multiply our sins. Sinful thoughts defile us even though they never come to actions. God hates sinful thoughts because sins of thought are the roots of sinful actions (Matthew 15:19). So, even if we commit no other sins at all, yet we need to repent of evil thoughts and beg pardon for them.

It is the great glory of the gospel message that it alone can bring our thoughts under the control of the message of Jesus Christ. The Holy Spirit uses his power to cleanse our spirits of what would otherwise defile them. His influence in a life and on the thoughts of a person has more power than any philosophy in the world. So the believer can say with the Apostle Paul,

> The weapons we fight with are not the weapons of the world. On the contrary, they have divine power to demolish strongholds. We demolish arguments and every pretension that sets itself up against the knowledge of God, and we take captive every thought to make it obedient to Christ (2 Corinthians 10:4 5).

The first step in a person's conversion takes place in their thoughts. Conversion is sometimes described as the renewing of the mind. Not only does conversion begin in the thoughts, it is also continued in the thoughts. The prayers of the godly are often taken up with the need for their thoughts to be cleansed (Psalm 51:10). Never forget that God will call us to account for our thoughts as well as our actions (Psalm 139:1 4).

There are practical things we can do in order to protect our thought life from sin:

Pray to God that past sins of thought may be forgiven and there may be no future ones.

Obey the instructions of God that you find in Scripture (e.g. Psalm 119:11).

Begin each day with thoughts of God and of good things.

Act quickly to rebuke wrong thoughts.

Keep a strict control on what you watch with your eyes.

Keep yourself busy doing good things.

Set your affections on godly things and godly behaviour.

In these ways I have tried to show the evil of sinful thoughts and to suggest ways we might seek to prevent them.

3. Beware of sinful words

Too many people think that it does not matter what they say. But Scripture makes it clear that our tongues are most difficult to control (James 3:7 8). Many lives can be damaged by unwise words: it is the person who can control the tongue who is wise (Proverbs 10:19; 21:23). Consider the following:

God has told us how we ought to speak (Ephesians 4:29: 5:4).

Talking much about religion does not make us a Christian (James 1:26).

Sinful words are evidence of sinful hearts (Psalm 12:1 2).

Evil words corrupt other people (James 3:5 6).

Our words are either our glory or our shame (Proverbs 10:20).

Idle words will have to be accounted for (Matthew 12:36 37).

So let me urge you to be careful with your words. God says, Let your words be few (Ecclesiastes 5:2). Silence often reveals wisdom. We should be swift to hear and slow to speak (James 1:19). When we speak, let us speak wholesome and true words. Be well in control of yourself before you speak, wrapping your words in silent prayer to God that they may be acceptable to him.

4. Beware of sinful actions

Before I speak in some detail about sinful actions I wish to speak about sins of omission — *failures* to act as we should. For it is wicked to omit to do any action which God has commanded.

> Even good people can neglect duties in private though performing them in public.
>
> If we are forced to omit duties by adverse circumstances, that should be a cause of sorrow to us.
>
> It is a sin to be willing to neglect a duty God has commanded. Too many people are glad of a diversion, like schoolboys when they can avoid studying. Often one omission will make way for another ... and another.
>
> The more knowledge we have of what we ought to do, the more aggravated and serious is the omission of that duty.
>
> To omit any duty in the sight of others is a serious wrong. A person may do much harm by not doing some good. There are biblical examples of those whom God has punished severely because they failed to do what they knew should be done — for example, Eli (1 Samuel 3:13) and the wicked servant (Matthew 25:26 30).

Clearly we will be judged for things we do not do as well as for what we have done. But to proceed further:

(i) Consider things we do which God forbids. There are particular sins we may be personally attracted to because we are most easily inclined to do them; popular sins of the age in which we live: sins of youth; sins of age; sins of the eyes; sins of relationships, husbands to wives and wives to husbands, child to parent, parent to child; sins of flattery, sins of unjust criticism; sins related to our daily work such as lying, fraud, corruption, denying agreements and dishonest trading. We can become involved in other people s sins, by not preventing them when we could. To tell a half truth is the same as telling a lie. In these and other ways we can quickly do many things which God forbids — sins of commission.

(ii) We ought to grieve whenever we see sinful acts, whether in ourselves or in others. We should speak out against what is sinful, lest God judge us guilty of that sin. We should always walk away from the presence of wickedness lest we be thought willing to condone it. I have dealt with these practical matters at some length because they are things that are not often spoken about.

As I come to the close of this book, may I entreat you to consider well what has been said and to realise what an ugly and damnable thing sin is. I have brought witnesses from heaven, earth and hell to prove that, and shown you how dearly it cost Jesus Christ, who died to save us from its power. Therefore I say: Stand in awe and do not sin!